FRANCE

BY YVETTE LaPIERRE

Essential Library

An Imprint of Abdo Publishing
abdobooks.com

ABDOBOOKS.COM

Published by Abdo Publishing, a division of ABDO, PO Box 398166, Minneapolis, Minnesota 55439. Copyright © 2023 by Abdo Consulting Group, Inc. International copyrights reserved in all countries. No part of this book may be reproduced in any form without written permission from the publisher. Essential Library™ is a trademark and logo of Abdo Publishing.

Printed in the United States of America, North Mankato, Minnesota.
102022
012023

Cover Photos: Shutterstock Images (Eiffel Tower, pattern)
Interior Photos: Luciano Mortula LGM/Shutterstock Images, 4–5; Lili Graphie/Shutterstock Images, 7; Shutterstock Images, 8, 12, 28–29, 30, 56, 61, 64, 65, 79, 83, 85, 86–87, 94; Ivan Soto Cobos/Shutterstock Images, 10–11; Andrew Mayovskyy/Shutterstock Images, 15; Gregory Dubus/iStockphoto, 16–17; Peter Hermes Furian/Shutterstock Images, 18 (France); Web Tools/Shutterstock Images, 18 (globe); Sergey Dzyuba/Shutterstock Images, 22; Roberto Caucino/Shutterstock Images, 24–25; Joost van Uffelen/Shutterstock Images, 27; Ali Alawartani/Shutterstock Images, 31; Bob Gibbons/Science Source, 33; Irina Kuzmina/Shutterstock Images, 37; Sylvain Thomas/AFP/Getty Images, 39; Pictures from History/Universal Images Group/Getty Images, 40–41; Stock Montage/Archive Photos/Getty Images, 43; Heritage Images/Hulton Fine Art Collection/Getty Images, 45; VCG Wilson/Fine Art/Corbis Historical/Getty Images, 48; Ullstein Bild Dtl./Getty Images, 50; Andia/Universal Images Group/Getty Images, 52, 91; Bruno Vigneron/Getty Images Entertainment/Getty Images, 54–55; Anna Klyasheva/Shutterstock Images, 62; Thomas Coex/AFP/Getty Images, 66–67; Bettmann/Getty Images, 69; Frederic Legrand-Comeo/Shutterstock Images, 71; Godong/Universal Images Group/Getty Images, 72; Daniel Mihailescu/AFP/Getty Images, 74; Thibaud Moritz/Abaca Press/Sipa USA/AP Images, 76–77; Adrian Nunez/Shutterstock Images, 80; Mara Ze/Shutterstock Images, 81; Claude Paris/AP Images, 82; Cliff Day/Shutterstock Images, 89; Nicolas Tucat/AFP/Getty Images, 92; Michel Euler/AP Images, 96–97; Crypto Skylark/Shutterstock Images, 101

Editor: Alyssa Sorenson
Series Designer: Maggie Villaume

Library of Congress Control Number: 2022940311

PUBLISHER'S CATALOGING-IN-PUBLICATION DATA

Names: LaPierre, Yvette, author.
Title: France / by Yvette LaPierre
Description: Minneapolis, Minnesota: Abdo Publishing, 2023 | Series: Essential Library of Countries | Includes online resources and index.
Identifiers: ISBN 9781532199400 (lib. bdg.) | ISBN 9781098274603 (ebook)
Subjects: LCSH: France--Juvenile literature. | Europe--Juvenile literature. | France--History--Juvenile literature. | Geography--Juvenile literature.
Classification: DDC 944.0--dc23

CONTENTS

A TOUR OF FRANCE

The moving walkway whisked the students through the busy Charles de Gaulle Airport in Paris, the capital of France. After the long trip from New York to France, everyone in the group was hungry. They decided to stop for a midmorning snack before gathering their bags and heading to the tour bus. The students were worried about using French that they had studied in class. They had heard French people could be rude sometimes. Madame Berry, their teacher, told them to do their best and be polite. She told them the French valued good manners. Most of the students ordered *pain au chocolat*. They had learned about this popular treat in class. The clerk

Paris is a busy city with more than two million people.

handed over the bag with a smile. When the students bit into the flaky pastries filled with chocolate, they understood why it was so popular.

When Madame Berry and her class were settled on the bus, they headed into Paris. The first stop was the most famous spot in the city: the Eiffel Tower. The students walked up the 360 steps to the first floor. They strolled along the outer walkway and admired the view of the city. They read informational signs that told them more about the Eiffel Tower. The class climbed more steps to the second floor. Hungry again, the students bought fancy French sandwich cookies at the macaron bar. They had learned in class that macarons became famous during the French Revolution (1787–1799). According to some historians, French nuns baked and sold the cookies during that time to support themselves.

The second floor of the Eiffel Tower had the best view of Paris. The students could see some of the city's famous landmarks, such as the Arc de Triomphe, the Notre-Dame Cathedral, and the Louvre Museum. They also could see the Seine River dividing the city in two. After a long wait in line, the students took an elevator up to the very top of the tower. The wind buffeted them as they stood 905.5 feet (276 m) above Paris.[1]

Back at the hotel, Madame Berry went over the trip's itinerary. They would spend the first few days in and around Paris. There was so much to see and do in the city that they couldn't possibly get to it all, but they would hit some highlights. These included the Louvre, the medieval fortress of Bastille, and the Palace of Versailles—the home of famous French kings and queens. Unfortunately, they would not be able to visit Notre-Dame Cathedral, which was more than 800 years old. It was still under construction after a devastating fire in 2019.

The students had been allowed to choose two outings. They had picked an afternoon of shopping at the Galeries Lafayette, a famous department store. The second outing was a spooky evening tour of the Catacombs of Paris. A guide would take them through the skull-and-bone-lined chamber. It was created in 1810 to deal with the city's overflowing cemeteries. The bones of millions of anonymous Parisians rested there. Madame Berry reminded the students that their backpacks would be searched as they left. The guards wanted to make sure that no visitors were stealing bones.

After Paris, the class would visit some other places in France. Among other sites, the students were eager to see the châteaus in the Loire Valley.

THE EIFFEL TOWER

Gustave Eiffel designed the Eiffel Tower for the 1889 world's fair. That year marked the one-hundredth anniversary of the French Revolution. The tower took 300 workers, 2.5 million rivets, 8,047 tons (7,300 metric tons) of iron, and more than two years to build.[3] When the tower was completed, it was the tallest human-made structure in the world at 1,063 feet (324 m) tall. Some people thought the tower was ugly and called it a "metal asparagus."[4] The Eiffel Tower was almost torn down in 1909. Today, millions of people visit this Paris icon every year.

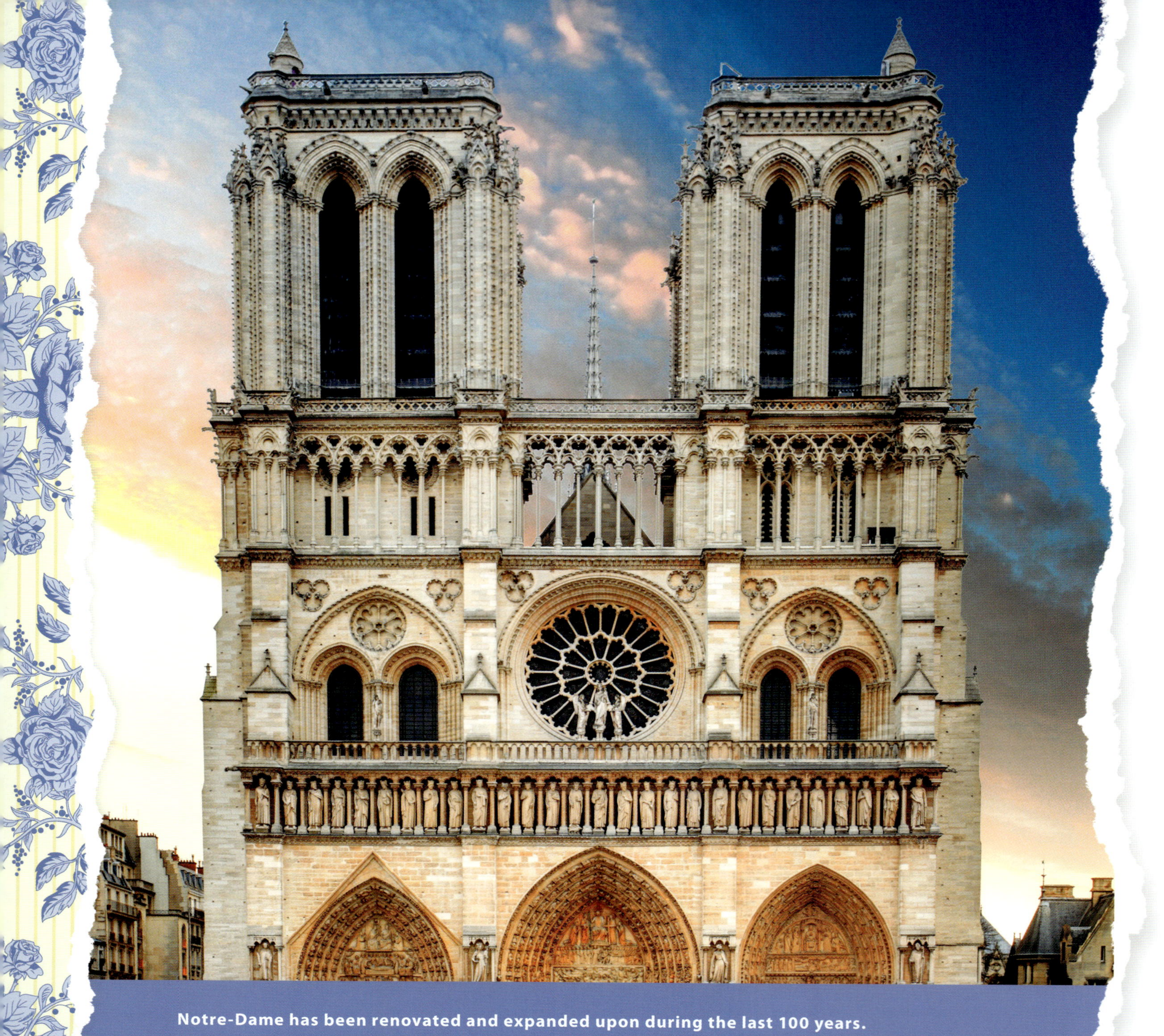

Notre-Dame has been renovated and expanded upon during the last 100 years.

Châteaus are historic castles or homes generally built in the country. The students also couldn't wait to see the old island city of Mont-Saint-Michel.

CHÂTEAUS OF THE LOIRE VALLEY

After a one-night stay in the city of Orléans, the bus brought Madame Berry and her class to the Loire Valley in west-central France. From their studies in class, the students knew that the beautiful Loire Valley was famous for its many châteaus built by France's kings, queens, and other nobility hundreds of years ago. It was also known for the wines made there. The students couldn't see all the castles in one day. Madame Berry chose tours of the two most famous: Château de Chenonceau and Château de Chambord. As the bus pulled up to Chenonceau, the students got their first glimpse of the elegant castle built on top of a bridge across a river. Inside, the students marveled at the long gallery over the river with a checkerboard floor.

The tour guide told the class that several women had been instrumental in building and protecting Chenonceau. The construction of the castle began in 1515 by a French aristocrat, but his

wife oversaw most of the design and building. Later, a king's mistress added the formal gardens outside. In the late 1700s, 83-year-old Madame Dupin saved the castle from being destroyed by an angry mob during the French Revolution. The tour guide also told the students that the castle had served as a hospital during World War II (1939–1945). Jewish people and resistance fighters found refuge there.

After a quick lunch in the tearoom, the class boarded the bus and headed to the grandest castle in the Loire Valley—the Château de Chambord. A tour guide led the students around some of the castle's 426 rooms and showed them the magnificent fireplaces and staircases.[5] The guide said the château's construction was started in 1519 by King Francis I. He wanted it to be a hunting retreat. Three decades later, it was the largest and grandest château in the valley. But the king decided it was too drafty and stayed there a total of only 72 days.

A highlight of the tour was walking up the double helix staircase. According to the guide, it was likely designed by the famous engineer, scientist, and artist Leonardo da Vinci. The students walked all the way to the top of the tower and onto the rooftop. From there, they gazed

King Francis I wanted the Château de Chambord to be a symbol of his power.

across the grounds. The guide told them that the hunting reserve was the largest walled park in Europe.

The bus took the students to the city of Blois for the night. Dinner was a hearty vegetable stew with a pastry crust and a plate of cheeses. A few students tried the cheeses, but most said they were too stinky. For dessert, they enjoyed an upside down apple tart known as tarte Tatin.

The students were tired but eager for the next day, when they would head north to visit even more stunning areas in France.

ABOUT FRANCE

France is located in western Europe, and it is a leader among other European nations. France is world-renowned for its beautiful mountains and beaches, high fashion and art, and delicious food and wine. France is one of the most visited countries in the world.

France borders the Bay of Biscay and the English Channel to the west and north, respectively. Also to the north lies the North Sea. The Mediterranean Sea is to the south. France shares borders with many countries. Belgium, Germany, Switzerland, Italy, and tiny Luxembourg lie to the east. Spain and the small nation of Andorra are to the southwest. France also shares a maritime, or water, border with the United Kingdom. France has long served as a bridge that joins the countries and cultures of northern and southern Europe.

Metropolitan, or mainland, France includes the land area in Europe plus the Mediterranean island Corsica. France also has control over five other islands. Its overseas regions are French Guiana in northeastern South America, the Caribbean islands Guadeloupe and Martinique, Mayotte in the western Indian Ocean, and Réunion off the coast of southeastern Africa. France has other dependent areas too, including French Polynesia and New Caledonia in the South Pacific.

France is one of the oldest nations in the world and has been an important country throughout its history. French ideals of democracy, science, art, and philosophy have spread throughout the globe. In the early 2020s, France was Europe's top agricultural country and a leader in industry. It has influence around the world as an important member of the European Union (EU), the North Atlantic Treaty Organization (NATO), and other multinational groups. Its capital city, Paris, is one of the world's greatest cultural and commercial centers.

Despite its rich natural resources and economic powers, the country faces ongoing challenges. Like most countries around the world, it was hit hard by the COVID-19 pandemic starting in 2020. The invasion of Ukraine by Russia in March 2022 created humanitarian and economic concerns throughout Europe. At the same time, France continued to confront the effects of climate change, immigration, and other global issues. France and its citizens would need to navigate these and other challenges to maintain leadership in Europe and the world.

CORSICA

Corsica is the fourth-largest island in the Mediterranean Sea. It lies 105 miles (170 km) from the southeastern tip of France. It is known as the Island of Beauty for its mountainous scenery, stone villages, and magnificent coastline. Corsica is also famous as the birthplace of the French emperor Napoléon Bonaparte in 1769.

More than 340,000 people live in Corsica.[6] Most live in the two biggest towns, Bastia and Ajaccio. French is the official language of Corsica, but most islanders also speak the Corsican dialect Corsu.

Many groups and countries have fought over Corsica since the 500s BCE. France invaded the island in 1768.

GEOGRAPHY

France is the largest country in western Europe and the third-largest country in all of Europe. Metropolitan France, which includes Corsica, covers 212,935 square miles (551,500 sq km). That's slightly smaller than the US state of Texas. When France's five overseas regions are included, the total area is 248,573 square miles (643,801 sq km).[1]

France is generally a flat country. It is covered by fertile plains and gentle hills. But the country also has majestic mountains, forested plateaus, and beautiful beaches.

Much of northern and western France is flat plains and rolling hills. The region includes several low-lying areas, or basins. The basins have rich soil, making them important agricultural centers. The Paris Basin is in

France is filled with rivers, mountains, and more.

MAP OF
FRANCE

KEY:

■ Capital

○ City

📍 Point of Interest

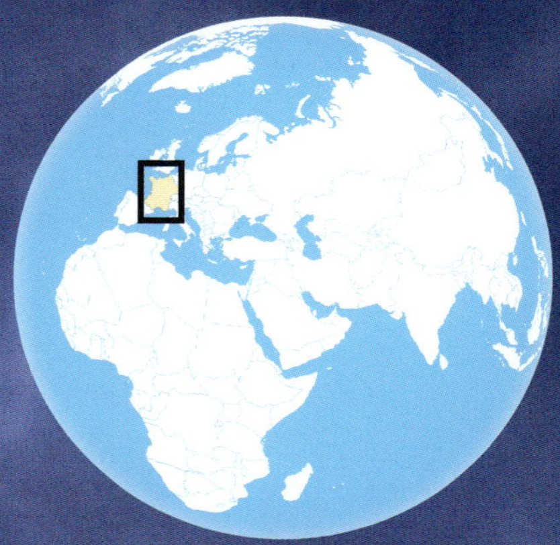

north-central France. Forests, grasslands, and fruit orchards cover the land. The Champagne region is in the eastern part of the basin. Its chalk plains and hills are famous for vineyards that produce sparkling wine.

Other lowland areas include the Aquitaine Basin in southwestern France, the Loire plains, and the Alsace Plain to the east. The Aquitaine Basin was once covered by heath and marshes but is now planted with pine trees. It includes the Bordeaux region, famous for its vineyards and wines.

The Loire plains follow the Loire River through the scenic valley known for its châteaus. Like many regions of France, the Alsace Plain's rich soil supports vineyards for making wine.

A sprawling, forested plateau dominates south-central France. It is known as the Massif Central, and it is the largest highland plateau in France. It covers approximately 33,000 square miles (86,000 sq km), which is about one-sixth of the entire area of the country.[2] The Massif Central is what's left of ancient mountain ranges that were worn down by weather over millions of years. The plateau has hot springs from past volcanic activity.

Just east of the Massif Central is the productive wine country of the Beaujolais region.

Mountains dominate the landscape in southern and eastern France. The Pyrenees mountain range stretches for hundreds of miles in southern France. It forms a natural border between France and Spain and Andorra. The snowy peaks and scenic valleys contain some of the best wilderness spots left in France. The French Alps are in southeastern France. They are part of a great mountain range that extends across Europe. The highest peak in the Alps is Mont Blanc, which rises 15,771 feet (4,807 m) above sea level in France.[4] The Alps are a popular destination for skiers and other winter tourists. Other smaller mountain ranges in France include the Jura Mountains and the Vosges range in the northeast.

Metropolitan France includes thousands of miles of coastlines and beautiful beaches and seashores. France's most famous coastline is the French Riviera, located in the southeast along the Mediterranean coast. It also is known as the Côte d'Azur. It includes some of Europe's most famous beaches, rocky coves, and resorts. It is a popular tourist destination.

RIVERS AND LAKES

France is ringed almost entirely by water and mountains. Many lakes can be found in the mountains. In addition, France has plains and coastal areas. The country's interior also has several major rivers that have shaped the land. France's river systems are divided roughly between the far eastern part of the country and the larger western part.

The major rivers in the east are the Rhine and the Rhône. Both rivers originate in the Alps. The Rhine River cuts through northeastern France on its way north to the North Sea. The Rhine also flows through Switzerland, Germany, and the Netherlands. It is one of Europe's longest rivers at 766 miles (1,233 km).[6]

The Rhône flows south and empties into the Mediterranean Sea. It is 505 miles (813 km) long and cuts through France and Switzerland.[7] It links Lake Geneva to the Alps and the Mediterranean Sea. Lake Geneva is a major freshwater lake on the north side of the Alps that lies in both France and Switzerland. It is 45 miles (72 km) long, 8.7 miles (14 km) wide, and as deep as 1,017 feet (310 m).[8] It is one of the largest freshwater lakes in Europe.

Major rivers west of the divide include the Garonne, the Loire, and the Seine. The Garonne originates in the Pyrenees in northern Spain. It flows over the southwestern border of France and north through the country into the Bay of Biscay. It is 357 miles (575 km) long.[9]

The Loire is the longest river in France at 629 miles (1,012 km).[10] It starts in the Massif Central highland plateau and flows north. It then bends to the west, flowing through the Loire Valley and to the Bay of Biscay.

The Seine is a well-known river that runs through Paris. The river starts in a northeastern plateau, flows through the Paris Basin, and then empties into the English Channel.

Throughout history, the Seine has been important to the economic development of Paris. It linked Paris with huge ports on the sea, bringing goods and people to the city. Currently, the Seine provides water for people, power stations, and industry in Paris and the surrounding region.

CLIMATE

France has a variety of climates. These change across the country and with the seasons. France can be divided into four broad climatic zones: mountain, oceanic, continental, and Mediterranean. The coldest places in France are in the high mountains. The mountain climate results in heavy rainfall and snow for three to six months of the year.

The oceanic climatic zone covers much of northwestern France. The region is generally humid with a moderate amount of rainfall. The temperature does not change too drastically between seasons. The average temperature is 43 degrees Fahrenheit (6°C) in January and 61 degrees Fahrenheit (16°C) in July.[11]

The continental zone dominates the plateaus and plains of the northeast. In general, the summers are hot and the winters cold. The northeastern city of Strasbourg near the German border has the greatest temperature range in France. Winters are very cold with snow and ice. Summers are warm with rainstorms in June and July. Average temperatures range from 31 degrees Fahrenheit (−0.5°C) in winter to 78 degrees Fahrenheit (25.5°C) in summer.[12]

The climate of the Paris Basin lies somewhere between the oceanic and continental zones. The average year-round temperature in Paris is 53 degrees Fahrenheit (11°C).[13] Rainfall in Paris

Some of the best winter skiing in France can be found in the Savoy region of the Alps.

is generally light but can occasionally be heavy in the spring, early summer, and fall.

The Mediterranean climate of southeastern France is hotter and drier than the rest of France with lots of sunshine. Fall and winter are damp but mild. However, southern France is subject to a violent wind known as the mistral. The wind may blow for many days with an average speed of 46 miles per hour (74 kmh) and can severely damage crops.[14]

FRANCE OVERSEAS

The five major overseas regions of France have a variety of landscapes and climates that differ from those of metropolitan France. French Guiana lies on the northeastern tip of South America and is the only French presence on that continent. Its landscape is mostly low-lying coastal plains that rise to hills and small mountains. The Amazon rain forest covers the majority of French Guiana. It is a tropical area with hot and humid weather and little variation in temperatures with seasons.

Guadeloupe is a group of islands in the Caribbean Sea. Martinique is another Caribbean island. These islands are mountainous and include dormant and active volcanoes. Coastlines are indented with bays that have beautiful beaches. The climate is subtropical with moderate humidity. Trade winds keep the temperatures from being too hot. The islands have a rainy season from June to October. Every few years, the islands may be hit by hurricanes.

Mayotte Island in the western Indian Ocean has a range of volcanic mountains. Bays dot the coastline, and coral reefs lie offshore. The weather is hot, humid, and rainy. The tropical climate supports lush evergreen forests.

The last main overseas region is the island of Réunion. The island is in the western Indian Ocean off the coast of southeastern Africa. Rugged mountains with high peaks dominate the landscape. Low fertile plains are found along the coast. Like Mayotte, it has a tropical climate. At higher elevations on the island, though, the weather is cooler and drier.

The French have claimed ownership over the island of Réunion since the mid-1600s.

PLANTS AND ANIMALS

France's broad climatic zones and varied landscapes support a rich diversity of plants and animals. The country has grassy plains and agricultural land, forested massifs and mountains, high alpine sections, and coastal lands. France is responsible for protecting the species living in both mainland France and its overseas regions and waters.

Metropolitan France has an estimated 54,766 plant and animal species. That represents 35 percent of the total number of species in all of Europe.[1] France is the most biologically diverse country in the EU.

France is committed to conservation efforts. The country's protection of plant and animal biodiversity

Many animals, such as the chamois, have adapted to survive on France's rugged landscapes.

dates back to the early 1960s when the first national parks were created. Since then, France has developed a number of action plans to protect endangered species and restore wilderness.

Despite that commitment, few habitats in France have escaped the negative effects of human impacts. These impacts include agriculture, city growth, wetland drainage, industry, and tourism. As a result, one in four species in France is endangered.[2]

ANIMALS

The varied environments of metropolitan France are home to more than 100 mammal species and more than 30 species of both reptiles and amphibians.[3] The high-elevation plains of the Alps and Pyrenees mountains are home to small populations of marmots, chamois, and Alpine ibex.

The Alpine ibex is the iconic animal of the French Alps, scrambling along the highest ledges of the mountain peaks. These wild goats have distinctive long horns that curve backward. Hunters prized these horns as trophies, and the ibex was hunted to near extinction across Europe in the 1500s. In the early 1900s, ibex were reintroduced in parts of the European Alps, including France. France created Vanoise National Park to help protect the animals. In the 2020s, ibex were thriving in the French Alps.

Marmots are large ground squirrels, and chamois are small but agile goat-antelopes that are native to France and other parts of Europe. Alpine ibex are wild goats with long, curved horns that live in the European Alps. In addition, wild mountain sheep called mouflons clamber over the high mountain slopes. Other high mountain species include alpine hares and rare brown bears.

Lowland forests are home to wild boars and deer. Red deer are common in the forested areas of northern France. Fallow deer can be found in the Massif Central. Roe deer are the smallest and most common species of deer in France. They thrive in many places, including the outskirts of big cities. Other common animals in France include red foxes, wildcats, and skunks. Hares and voles are abundant in the country, as are several species of mink and marten. The gray wolf became extinct in France in the 1930s. Wolves were reintroduced in 1992 and are now protected from hunting and trapping. France also is home to marine mammals. Dolphins and whales can be spotted in the Mediterranean Sea near the Côte d'Azur and Corsica.

Birds living in France include starlings, thrushes, robins, and rooks. Other birds include ptarmigan, nutcrackers, black grouse, and three-toed woodpeckers. White storks build nests on the roofs and in chimneys of buildings in the Alsace region of northeastern France. The Mediterranean coastline is a popular stopover for millions of migrating birds. It attracts rollers, bee-eaters, ducks, and geese, among others. Birds of prey in France include hawks, kestrels, buzzards, and rare golden eagles and eagle owls. Europe's largest bird of prey—the bearded vulture—lives in metropolitan France.

The Camargue is a large wetland in southern France. The marshy area is where the Rhône River empties into the sea. It attracts hundreds of bird species, including egrets, herons, and thousands of pink flamingos. It is the only region in western Europe where these birds nest.

PLANTS

France's climates and soils support a variety of plant life. Along the dry, sandy soils of the coasts grow conifers, olives, and live oaks. Chestnuts and cork oaks grow in both the Mediterranean region of France and on the island of Corsica. Small shrubs and herbs dominate the hot, dry coastlines of the Côte d'Azur and Corsica. These plants are low growing with small leaves, deep

Cork oak tree bark is used to make cork bottles.

roots, and thick bark. These characteristics help the plants conserve water during droughts. The Atlantic coast supports hardy plants such as broom, furze, and heather.

Forests cover approximately 54,000 square miles (140,000 sq km) of France, or roughly 20 percent of the country.[4] Many of the trees in the forests are deciduous trees, which lose their leaves in the winter. The most common trees are beeches and oaks. Other trees include maples, chestnuts, and ashes.

Higher elevations with colder winters in northern and eastern France support different trees, shrubs, and flowers. Pines, spruces, and firs dominate mountain slopes on the Pyrenees and Alps between 2,625 feet (800 m) and 4,929 feet (1,500 m) high.[5] Above that elevation grow shrubs and smaller trees, such as larch, pines, rhododendrons, and junipers.

Colorful wildflowers carpet the high alpine meadows in spring and summer. Some of the native wildflowers include the purple alpine columbine, the flame-colored fire lily, and the bright-yellow arnica. Other alpine wildflowers include gentians, yellow pasqueflowers, and alpine pansies. Edelweiss grows in the French Alps.

PROTECTED AREAS

Some of the land in both mainland France and its overseas regions is protected by a system of national parks, regional parks, and nature reserves. France has 11 national parks, and three of those are in overseas territories. The national park system protects about 10 percent of metropolitan France. Some nine million people visit the parks each year.[6]

Vanoise National Park in mainland France was established in 1963 and protects stunning mountain peaks and valleys rich with wildlife. Port-Cros National Park off the coast of southeastern

France also was created in 1963. It is the oldest land-and-sea park in Europe. France's largest national park is the Guiana Amazonian Park. It covers a chunk of French Guiana and preserves one of the planet's most biodiverse places.

Dozens of regional parks protect land in metropolitan France and its territories. Two were added in 2020. One of these was Somme Bay in northern France. The other was a mountain called Mont Ventoux in southeastern France. The country also has hundreds of smaller nature reserves.

Some areas of France are protected as United Nations Educational, Scientific, and Cultural Organization (UNESCO) World Heritage sites. The sites are picked for their unique and significant value. For example, the Gulf of Porto site covers a stretch of land and water along Corsica's west coast. The 30,000-acre (12,140 ha) site includes dramatic red cliffs, black volcanic rock, hidden marine caves, and bright-blue waters.[7] The clear water hosts rich marine wildlife, including dolphins and seals, and waterbirds such as seagulls, cormorants, and osprey. The Mont Perdu site in the Pyrenees protects some of the stunning mountain landscape in the area. The site spans the borders of France and Spain and centers on a peak that is 10,997 feet (3,352 m) high.[8]

HUMAN IMPACTS

France's biodiversity is threatened by a number of human activities. These activities include climate change, pollution, habitat loss, and overuse of natural resources, such as overfishing. Urbanization and intense farming destroy the habitats of many plants and animals. In addition, the use of herbicides and pesticides harms wildlife. For example, pesticide use is mostly to blame for the decrease in the numbers of common birds in mainland France. The population of birds such as swallows decreased by 22 percent between 1989 and 2017 due in large part to people using pesticides.[9]

Acid rain is caused by air pollution from industrial and vehicle emissions. It damages trees and forests. Agricultural runoff and urban waste pollute water that wildlife depend on. In addition, wildfires burn large areas of forest every summer. Some are started accidentally, but arsonists are also responsible for a portion of France's wildfires. Since the mid-1970s, there have been hundreds of recorded wildfires each year.

People have different ways of describing how much danger a species is in. They may use the

The Gulf of Porto has some of the most dramatic landscapes on Corsica.

terms *vulnerable*, *threatened*, and *near threatened*. A vulnerable classification means that a species faces a high likelihood of becoming extinct in the wild. Threatened species are likely to become endangered in the future. Near threatened means that a species is close to gaining a threatened status. Of the total number of plant and animal species evaluated by a French conservation organization, at least 8 percent are near threatened.[10] Furthermore, an estimated 26 percent of France's species are vulnerable.[11]

France's overseas territories also have their share of threatened species. Of France's total number of endangered plant and animal species, 39 percent live on overseas islands. These islands contain 86 percent of France's endemic species, or species that don't live elsewhere on Earth.[12] Many of these species are particularly vulnerable to climate change.

Perhaps the most endangered species in France and all of Europe is the European mink. Minks live in rivers in the middle of forests and hunt fish, frogs, and crustaceans. The biggest factor in their decline is competition from American minks, which were introduced to Europe in the 1920s. Minks also are threatened by habitat loss, hunting, and pollution.

More than 19,000 plant and animal species are endemic to France and its territories.[13]

Another highly endangered mammal that lives in France's waters is the North Atlantic right whale. Only a few hundred are alive in the world. Many whales drown when they get tangled up in fishing gear. Their decline also is due to climate

Firefighters in France work hard to stop wildfires from consuming large areas of habitat.

change and heightened levels of ocean noise. Other increasingly rare mammals in France include beavers, brown bears, and mouflons.

Coral reefs face threats from climate change too. France is responsible for coral reefs in multiple oceans where its overseas territories are located. As the ocean waters change, coral reef surfaces are getting damaged and are dying.

CHAPTER FOUR

HISTORY

People have lived in what is now southwestern France for at least 54,000 years. Early people lived in caves and hunted large animals. They left many artifacts, including paintings on cave walls. During the Iron Age, which started around 1200 BCE, different groups of people began migrating to northwestern France. The largest of these groups were Celtic Gauls. For the next 1,000 years, they spread throughout the region, farming and raising livestock. The Gauls brought iron tools and weapons with them, and they built the first villages and communities in France. The Gauls were divided into many separate tribes with their own territories.

The small tribes were not united, which made them vulnerable to invasions by outsiders. The Romans first

Lascaux cave in southwestern France has prehistoric paintings that are around 20,000 years old.

conquered part of southern France in 121 BCE and named it a province of the Roman Empire. By 50 BCE, the Romans had conquered the whole region. The Gauls slowly adopted Roman ways of life, including planting vineyards and making wine.

By the mid-200s CE, the Roman Empire was weakening. As it declined, German tribes invaded France. The most successful were part of a group known as the Franks. They ruled northern France by approximately 500. The greatest Frankish ruler was Charlemagne. From 768 until his death in 814, he expanded the Frankish Empire until it had taken over most of western Europe. Upon his death, the empire was divided into three parts. The western part became known as the kingdom of France.

HUNDRED YEARS' WAR

French kings had little power over most of France in the early years of the kingdom. Local nobility, including counts and dukes, ruled their individual parts of the country. In 1066, the French Duke of Normandy invaded and conquered England. Later, English kings claimed parts of France. This rivalry between France and England lasted for 300 years.

Joan of Arc believed that God was guiding her to help France and fight the English. She is revered as a holy person in the Catholic Church.

The longest period of fighting started in 1337. France and England fought on and off until the mid-1400s. It became known as the Hundred Years' War (1337–1453). At one point, France was close to total defeat. A young peasant girl named Joan of Arc led the French army to victory. After that, the tide of war changed. The English lost nearly all the land they had claimed in France by the end of the war in 1453.

At the time, France was a Roman Catholic nation. During the 1500s, Protestant Christianity began to spread throughout the country. This led to wars between Catholics and Protestants. In 1598, King Henry IV granted Protestants some rights, and the fighting stopped.

During the 1500s, the French population was growing quickly, and the country was becoming richer. France became the greatest power in Europe. Art and philosophy flourished. Scientific discoveries were made. Architects designed stunning cathedrals and palaces, including the châteaus in the Loire Valley. This artistic and cultural movement lasted from the late 1400s to the early 1600s and was known as the French Renaissance.

During this period, French kings gained greater power and wealth. By the end of the 1600s, France was an absolute monarchy, meaning the French king or queen had total control over the government. France's King Louis XIV reigned from 1643 to 1715 and is a symbol of the absolute monarch. He strived to control everything from army movements to court etiquette. Louis XIV built the extravagant Palace of Versailles and allowed France to engage in a lot of costly wars.

FRENCH REVOLUTION

France was a hotbed of political and intellectual thought in the 1700s. This period, which lasted from around 1601 to 1800, was known as the Age of Enlightenment. One famous French thinker of the time was Voltaire, who promoted new ideas of democracy and free speech. Also during the 1700s, French kings continued to spend money on costly foreign wars, including the American Revolution (1775–1783). France declared war on Great

ÉMILIE DU CHÂTELET

Émilie du Châtelet was a mathematician, physicist, and author—all impressive accomplishments for a woman in the 1700s. Du Châtelet was born on December 17, 1706, in Paris. Her father was an aristocrat who often invited scientists to his home. He recognized his daughter's intelligence at an early age and encouraged her scientific ambitions. He hired tutors to teach her languages, math, literature, and science.

Du Châtelet married when she was 19 years old. After the birth of her three children, du Châtelet continued her studies in algebra, calculus, and physics. She published scientific articles and translations.

Du Châtelet died in September 1749, shortly after giving birth to her fourth child. That same year, she had completed her masterpiece. It was a translation of the famous English mathematician and physicist Isaac Newton's *Principia Mathematica*. Du Châtelet's was the first and only translation into French of that groundbreaking work for a long time.

As an adult, Émilie du Châtelet conducted experiments in energy conservation.

Britain in support of the American colonists. The war was expensive, and France had to borrow a lot of money. The kings also raised taxes on French citizens to finance these wars.

Some French people prospered during the 1700s, but many remained terribly poor. Public anger grew at the money spent on lavish palaces and foreign wars. By the late 1780s, King Louis XVI and Queen Marie-Antoinette were living an extravagant lifestyle, completely out of touch with the lives of their citizens. Public anger reached a boiling point, and a wave of unrest and frustration with the wealthy swept the entire country. On July 14, 1789, ordinary people in Paris seized weapons and stormed the Bastille. This state prison was a symbol of the monarchy. The French Revolution had started. The motto of the revolutionaries was "Liberty, Equality, Fraternity."[2]

In August, the Declaration of the Rights of Man and of the Citizen was adopted by a governing body that represented French citizens. The declaration said that all men are born free and equal. By August 1792, the royal family was imprisoned. King Louis XVI was put on trial and executed in January 1793. Marie-Antoinette was executed that October. The monarchy had ended, and France became a republic.

NAPOLÉON BONAPARTE

The new French Republic faltered after a short period. General Napoléon Bonaparte began to rise to power at the end of the 1700s after leading France to a series of victories over foreign enemies. In 1804, he declared himself emperor of France and set out on an ambitious plan to conquer Europe.

An emperor is essentially the same as a king, though Napoléon continued to uphold some of the changes of the French Revolution, including the idea of equality for all men. He didn't return France to a nation of privileged nobility living lavish lifestyles. He did, however, undermine other gains made during the French Revolution. He introduced censorship of the press and imprisonment without a trial. He also reduced women's rights.

By 1812, Napoléon had much of Europe under his control. But several countries banded together to stop his armies. In 1815, he was defeated by a combined British and Dutch force at the Battle of Waterloo in what is now Belgium.

After Napoléon's defeat, a series of unpopular monarchs ruled France. Citizens rioted, and the Second Republic began in 1848. Napoléon's nephew was elected president but then declared himself emperor. In 1870, the French people again revolted against their ruler, and France established the Third Republic. It has been a republic ever since.

The 1870s ushered in a period known as the Belle Époque, or the "Beautiful Age" (1871–1914). It was a time of peace and relative prosperity for many people in France. There were advances in science and engineering, as well as artistic movements. Important artistic trends from the

Napoléon Bonaparte was exiled from France twice—once in 1814 and again in 1815 after he lost the Battle of Waterloo.

time include Art Nouveau architecture and furnishings. The Art Nouveau style was deliberately created as a way to break free from old artistic traditions. In architecture, the style took inspiration from the natural world and included decorations of vines, flowers, and animals, as well as curving lines and arches. The Belle Époque was also a period when artists experimented with Impressionist paintings.

THE WORLD WARS

This period of peace and prosperity ended when Germany invaded France in 1914 during World War I (1914–1918). More than one million French soldiers died in the war, and almost as many were left with physical disabilities.[3] Buildings, roads, and other infrastructure were destroyed. This left France heavily in debt and with a greatly weakened economy. France and its allies defeated Germany, and World War I ended in 1918.

France's economy began to recover in the early 1920s. In 1929, however, the New York stock market crash triggered a global economic depression that affected many countries, including France. While the French government tried to dig its country out of the depression, the politician Adolf Hitler and his Nazi Party were rising to power in Germany. Hitler began to take over nearby countries, and France decided not to get involved in the conflicts. It wasn't until Germany invaded Poland in September 1939 that France and the United Kingdom decided to take action, and World War II began. The following May, Germany invaded France. After just six weeks, France surrendered to Germany on June 22, 1940.

Nazi Germany occupied northern and eastern France, including Paris. Germany took France's resources, including industrial goods, crops, and livestock. Hundreds of thousands of French people were forced to go to Germany to work. Many French citizens were imprisoned and killed as part of the Holocaust orchestrated by the Nazis. The Holocaust was the genocide of millions of people, most of them Jewish. Many French people who remained in France went hungry.

Part of the French army managed to escape to England. French general Charles de Gaulle led these soldiers, known as the Free French. US, British, and Free French armies finally drove the German soldiers out of France in 1944. De Gaulle became the president of the newly liberated Fourth Republic of France.

POSTWAR FRANCE

France's economy recovered after the war and began growing in the 1950s and 1960s. The French government invested in automobile factories, oil and gas exploration, and other industries. It began building hydroelectric and nuclear power plants to support the nation's growing industry and population. As France grew, so did its political power around the world.

In 1958, France passed a new constitution and established the Fifth Republic. De Gaulle continued as president until he resigned in 1969. In 1981, France elected its first socialist president. President François Mitterrand strengthened government-sponsored social programs for all citizens and reduced the number of working hours.

Throughout the late 1900s and early 2000s, France continued to grow in economic prosperity and power as a world leader. France became one of the original members of the EU in 1993. In 1999, France joined more than a dozen other EU countries to adopt a common currency, the euro. The country weathered economic difficulties during this time too. There were periods of high unemployment and government debt. Public protests led to changes in government spending and public policies.

People set up a memorial after the November 2015 terrorist attacks.

This period also saw a rise in terrorist attacks. France suffered two major attacks in 2015. One attack happened in January. Islamic extremists attacked a magazine office. In November, multiple coordinated attacks by suicide bombers and gunmen terrorized different spots in Paris. Overall, more than 130 people were killed, and hundreds of others were injured.[4] On July 14, 2016—a day of national celebration in France—a terrorist struck the city of Nice. He was from North Africa and had moved to France. Some people said he had ties to the Islamic State, though investigators found no solid link. Nevertheless, the attack led to anti-immigration sentiments among some French people.

During the presidential election in 2017, two candidates advanced to a final runoff. One was a conservative candidate, Marine Le Pen, who ran on a platform of severely restricting immigration and limiting France's role in the EU. The other candidate was centrist Emmanuel Macron, who supported France's ties to the EU and economic reform. Macron easily won the runoff, becoming the youngest president ever elected in France, at 39 years old.

Macron implemented many economic reforms, though not all were popular. In 2018 and 2019, Macron faced many protests from people who were unhappy with his plans to raise certain taxes, reform pension plans, and increase working hours. Macron was also committed to tackling global climate change and limiting France's emissions of greenhouse gases. Macron's government introduced national measures to ban single-use plastic bags in the country and to stop selling all gas- and diesel-powered vehicles by 2040.

Terror attacks continued into the 2020s. Other significant issues facing Macron's government included the COVID-19 pandemic and the Russian invasion of Ukraine. In 2020, France celebrated its republic's 150th anniversary.

CHAPTER FIVE

PEOPLE AND CULTURE

More than 68 million people lived in France and its five overseas regions in 2022, and the country's population was steadily growing. Of those people, nearly 63 million lived in metropolitan France. Adults aged 25 and older made up almost 70 percent of France's population. The country's citizens had a life expectancy of 79 years for men and almost 86 years for women.[1]

The most populous regions of the country are in the southeast and north, which includes Paris—by far the largest city in France. Paris has more than two million people.[2] Lyon in east-central France is the

In early December every year, Lyon holds the Fête des Lumières, or "Festival of Lights," for a few nights. People set up dazzling light shows and decorate the city with art.

Marseille is one of the biggest cities in France, with more than one million people living there.

second-largest city. Other populous regions include the southern cities of Marseille and Toulouse, and Lille in the north, near Belgium.

The majority of France's population lives in cities. Throughout most of its history, however, France was a rural nation, and French people lived on farms and in small villages. Larger communities, including Paris, began to develop in the Middle Ages. By 1500, Paris was Europe's largest city. People began leaving rural villages for cities in large numbers during the Industrial Revolution of the 1700s and 1800s. France has been an urban nation since then.

ETHNIC MIX AND LANGUAGES

The region now known as France was settled by groups of people who spread throughout Europe. Celtic people, who were called Gauls by the Romans, came from central Europe to central and western France in the period from 500 BCE to 500 CE. The region was conquered by the Romans. After the fall of the Roman Empire in the 400s CE, Teutonic, or Germanic, people spread through France. Among the earliest migrants to the region were the Basque people, small populations of whom still live in the Pyrenees in both France and Spain.

Immigration in the 1800s and 1900s contributed more ethnic diversity to France. France has minority populations of Slavic, North African, and Indo-Chinese people. The ethnic mix of France's overseas regions also includes sub-Saharan African, East Indian, Chinese, and Amerindian people.

French is the official language of France. It is spoken by 125 million people around the world, and it was the official language of the EU until 1995.[3] French people once spoke a number of regional dialects and languages, including Basque. Basque is a language unrelated to French and other European languages. Basque and other dialects have declined greatly, and almost all French people speak standard French. In the overseas regions, a Jamaican dialect called Creole patois and a Swahili dialect called Mahorian are spoken in addition to French.

French people practice a number of religions, but France is a secular state. That means the nation does not support any particular religious belief and that there is a strict division between religion and the government. A French law prohibits the government from collecting information on its citizens' religious beliefs. It is difficult, therefore, to report accurate data on how many people practice a certain religion. It's estimated that almost half of the population belongs to the Roman Catholic Church. France has one of Europe's largest Muslim populations, estimated at 4 percent. Other religions represented in France include Protestantism, Buddhism, and Judaism. One-third of the population is not religious.[4]

FINE ARTS

France has a deep and rich history in the arts, from visual art and architecture to ballet and fashion. France has been home to many famous artists throughout history, including sculptor Auguste Rodin, illustrator Henri de Toulouse-Lautrec, and painter Rosa Bonheur. Rodin's 1902 masterpiece is the bronze sculpture of a male figure who appears in deep thought, called *The Thinker*. Toulouse-Lautrec depicted scenes of Paris nightlife in the late 1800s, including a cancan dancer at the popular nightclub the Moulin Rouge. Bonheur made stunning paintings of animals that were noticed by the French empress in 1865.

French painter Claude Monet was the founder of the art movement known as Impressionism in the 1860s. He used dabs of color to suggest shapes and light. Some of his best-known paintings were of water lilies, fields with haystacks, and the Rouen Cathedral. Other important French Impressionists include Édouard Manet, Berthe Morisot, and Eva Gonzalès.

In addition to artists and artistic movements, France is famous for its museums. The Louvre in Paris contains one of the world's greatest collections of art. It displays tens of thousands of works of art, from ancient Egyptian and Greek artifacts to European masterpieces by the sculptor Michelangelo; the painter Rembrandt; and the artist, scientist, and engineer Leonardo da Vinci. The most popular piece of art at the Louvre is da Vinci's *Mona Lisa*. Other important museums in Paris include the Pompidou Center, which holds Europe's largest collection of modern and contemporary art, and the Musée d'Orsay, which has a large collection of art from the 1800s and 1900s. Some of the museum buildings themselves are considered works of art.

France's museums, cathedrals, châteaus, and public buildings showcase a variety of architectural styles and innovations. French architects helped create architectural movements, including Beaux-Arts, Art Deco, and Gothic. Beaux-Arts buildings are influenced by classical Greek and Roman architecture. Art Deco originated in France in the 1920s and was known for clean, modern lines and shapes.

The most famous example of Gothic architecture is Notre-Dame Cathedral. It was built in the late 1100s and early 1200s as France was becoming a nation and Paris was becoming the largest city in Europe. The new Gothic style included tall, pointed arches; flying buttresses; and enormous stained-glass windows. The cathedral, a masterpiece of Gothic architecture, has survived for eight centuries, through fires, riots, and neglect.

France also developed the dance form known as ballet. Ballet combines dance with music, costume, and plot to tell a story. The first ballet was performed at the French Court in 1581. King Louis XIV established what is now known as the Paris Opera Ballet in 1661. Louis XIV also helped define the extravagant clothing style of French royalty, and eventually France became known as the fashion capital of the world. French citizens rejected lavish clothes after the Revolution, but high fashion returned in the early 1900s. Some of France's famous fashion houses include Chanel, Christian Dior, and Louis Vuitton. France continues to host fashion shows and help set new clothing trends.

Late 1900s innovations in French architecture include the pyramid entrance to the Louvre.

FOOD

France is known for its delicious food, and many of the greatest chefs have trained there. People consider French cuisine to be an art form. Some of the country's famous delicacies include escargot, which is snails cooked in garlic butter; foie gras, which is goose or duck liver; and crepes,

which are thin and delicate pancakes stuffed with sweet or savory fillings. Rich sauces made from butter, cream, or wine accompany many meat, fish, and vegetable dishes.

The most popular food in France, however, is bread. Almost every city, town, and small village across France has its own boulangerie, or bakery. A trip to the bakery for fresh baguettes is practically a daily ritual in France. Patisserie, or pastry shops, sell sweeter breads and treats. These include brioche, flaky croissants, tarts, petits fours, and macarons.

The French are known for their love of cheese, and they enjoy many different kinds. In fact, France produces more than 500 cheese varieties, and many are sold and eaten all over the world.[7] Some of the best-known varieties include Camembert, Brie, and Roquefort.

The French have been making wine since Roman times, and they have developed varieties recognized around the world. Many famous French wines are known for the region where the grapes are grown. For example, the red wines burgundy and bordeaux are produced in those areas of the country. Sparkling wines have been produced in the Champagne region northeast of Paris since the 1600s. Only sparkling wines made with grapes from this region in the traditional way can legally be called champagne.

The French enjoy eating out in restaurants and cafés and lingering over a cup of coffee or glass of wine while talking with friends and family, as they have for centuries. The oldest restaurant in Paris, now known as Le Procope, opened in 1686. It was a gathering place for people to meet and discuss science, philosophy, and current events. A few of the famous people who dined there include Napoléon Bonaparte, the French writer Victor Hugo, the philosopher Voltaire, and Benjamin Franklin, a Founding Father of the United States.

SPORTS AND RECREATION

The most famous sporting event in France is the Tour de France bicycle race, which has attracted the world's best male cyclists since the first race in 1903. The race also draws in millions of spectators, who line the streets to cheer on the cyclists. In the Tour de France, teams of nine cyclists pedal a course that's approximately 2,000 miles (3,200 km) long. It lasts for three weeks and consists of one-day-long stages. The course covers various terrains, including the Alps and the Pyrenees. Sometimes it crosses into such countries as Belgium, Italy, Germany, and Spain. But the race always ends on the Champs-Élysées—a street in Paris.

Auto racing is another popular spectator sport in France. The two most famous auto races are Le Mans and the Grand Prix in Monaco. In addition, French people enjoy a number of other organized sports, including tennis and soccer. In 1998, France hosted the soccer World Cup and won. Skiing is also popular in France's many high mountain resorts.

HOLIDAYS AND CELEBRATIONS

A number of public holidays and festivals take place in France. July 14 is a day of national celebration. It marks the end of the monarchy and the beginning of the modern republic. Commonly referred to as Bastille Day, it commemorates the storming of the Bastille in 1789 during the French Revolution. The main event of Bastille Day is a grand parade along the Champs-Élysées that is attended by the French president, other political leaders, and thousands of citizens. Cities and towns across the country celebrate with fireworks and dances.

The French celebrate several seasonal and religious holidays, including New Year's Day, Easter, May Day, and Christmas. A popular celebration is Mardi Gras, which means "Fat Tuesday" in French

WOMEN'S TOUR DE FRANCE

For most of its long history, France's famous Tour de France bike race was exclusively for men. In 1984, the first women's Tour de France debuted, but it ended in 1989. The Tour de France Femmes made a comeback in the summer of 2022. The eight-day race started at the Eiffel Tower and covered 639 miles (1,028 km) of mountains and flat landscapes.

Thousands of troops from the French military march during the Bastille Day parade.

and marks the beginning of the Christian season of Lent. Mardi Gras is celebrated with street parties, parades, and food. One of the world's largest and oldest Mardi Gras carnivals is held in Nice in southeastern France along the French Riviera. France hosts a number of other cultural events, including the Cannes Film Festival, wine harvest festivals in Alsace, and World Music Day.

CHAPTER SIX

POLITICS

The official name for France is the French Republic. The name comes from the Latin word *Francia*, which means "Land of the Franks." The name of France's capital city, Paris, comes from a Celtic word. A Celtic tribe called the Parisii lived in the area starting in 200 BCE. The Celtic settlement was then replaced by a Roman town, but the city name retained its Celtic roots.

France has a history of different rulers and government structures. These include monarchies, empires, and republics. France's current government is known as the Fifth Republic.

France's National Assembly meets in the Palais Bourbon in Paris to discuss and pass laws.

GOVERNMENT

The Constitution of the Fifth Republic was approved on October 4, 1958. It was based on a set of principles laid out by General Charles de Gaulle during a speech he gave in June 1946 following Germany's occupation of France in World War II. The constitution reestablished France as a republic. This is a form of government in which a state is ruled by representatives who are elected by the citizens. France divides its government into three branches: an executive branch, a legislative branch, and a judicial branch.

The executive branch consists of the president and the prime minister. Citizens elect the president, or head of state, by a majority vote. The president serves a five-year term and is eligible for a second term. The president appoints the prime minister. The prime minister serves as the head of government and leads a group of officials known as the Council of Ministers. The ministers are appointed by the president at the recommendation of the prime minister. The ministers are in charge of the nation's daily operations, including the economy, foreign affairs, defense, education, and justice. Each minister heads a department. Examples of

MODERN DEMOCRACY

Some historians call both France and the United States the birthplaces of modern democracy. In France during the 1600s and 1700s, French thinkers and philosophers gathered to discuss the ideals of democracy and individual freedoms. One was the famous French writer and philosopher Voltaire. The United States' Benjamin Franklin spent time with Voltaire and brought these ideas back to the colonies. The success of the American Revolution helped prove that the democratic ideals developed in France could work in practice.

CHARLES DE GAULLE

Charles de Gaulle was a French general and statesman, and he was one of the country's most important political leaders in the modern era. De Gaulle was born on November 22, 1890. He entered the military and served in the French army during World War I. After the war, he wrote many books and articles on military subjects.

When Germany invaded France at the beginning of World War II, de Gaulle was strongly opposed to France's surrender. He escaped to the United Kingdom, where he set up a provisional French government and led the Free French forces to liberate France. After the country was freed from German rule in 1944, de Gaulle helped guide the country through the postwar years and the adoption of a new constitution.

De Gaulle became France's prime minister in 1958. He became president in January 1959. He worked to make France the dominant economic and military power in Europe.

Charles de Gaulle proved himself a capable military leader before entering politics.

departments include the Ministry of the Interior, the Ministry for Overseas France, and the Ministry of National Education, Youth and Sports.

The French Parliament forms the legislative, or lawmaking, branch. The Parliament consists of two bodies: the National Assembly and the Senate. The National Assembly is the more powerful body and has 577 members. Its members are elected directly by citizens in a majority vote. The Senate has 348 elected seats. Citizens of France's overseas territories elect their own officials. These territories have much independence in making political and legislative decisions. Some issues, however, remain under executive control, such as diplomacy and national defense. France has many political parties, including the Republic on the Move, the Republicans, the Democratic Movement, and the Socialist Party.

The third arm of government is the judicial branch. It decides on the meaning of laws and applies justice when laws are broken. The French courts have two separate parts: the administrative and the judicial courts. The administrative courts deal with public law and settle lawsuits brought up by local and state bodies and individuals. The judicial courts deal with civil and criminal laws.

HÔTEL MATIGNON'S GARDEN

The official residence of the prime minister in Paris is known as Hôtel Matignon. The house is impressive, but many people enjoy the garden even more. French prime ministers have shaped the garden since 1725. Some highlights are a magnificent purple beech tree that is 150 years old and two ivy-covered tombstones for a dog and a cat buried there long ago. Since 1978, each new prime minister has picked a tree to plant along a curved pathway in the garden.

Emmanuel Macron became France's president in 2017.

POLITICAL SYMBOLS

France's political symbols—both official and unofficial—grew out of the French Revolution and its ideals. Those ideals are summarized in the French national motto: "Liberty, Equality, Fraternity." The French flag features three broad stripes of blue, white, and red. White was traditionally the

Marianne represents liberty, equality, and fraternity.

color of the French monarchy. Blue and red were the colors of the Parisian army. The tricolor flag had been used by the French people before the French Revolution and was adopted by the French government in 1794.

"La Marseillaise" became the official national anthem in 1958. The song was composed in April 1792 as a marching song. The Marseille troops sang it as they entered Paris on July 30, 1792. This song helped rally the citizens of Paris and became an anthem of the French Revolution.

Citizens adopted the fictional Marianne as the unofficial symbol of the motherland during the Revolution. Marianne is depicted as a young woman dressed as a warrior, symbolizing that mothers are at times fierce and warlike to protect their children. Marianne also is a symbol of liberty, which is something to be fought for. The symbol is an ancient one. Marianne wears a bonnet that was worn by freed slaves during the Roman Empire. Town halls in cities across France display busts of Marianne wearing her bonnet.

The Gallic rooster is an unofficial symbol of the French Republic. In Latin, *gallus* means both "rooster" and "inhabitant of Gaul," the Roman name for France. Citizens began using the rooster as a symbol of the emerging nation during the French Revolution. During his reign, Napoléon replaced the rooster with the more powerful eagle. But during World War I, the Gallic rooster became a symbol of France's bravery in the face of the eagle crest of Prussia, a former German state.

MILITARY

France's military consists of an army, navy, air and space force, and national guard. The country also has a National Gendarmerie, which serves as France's law enforcement. The army is France's largest and best-equipped defense force. It has about 205,000 active duty troops. The National Gendarmerie has around 100,000 active duty troops, and the National Guard has approximately 75,000.[1]

In 2022, European stability was threatened after Russia invaded Ukraine. In response, France sent military troops and equipment to Romania—a NATO ally—to help deter any potential acts of aggression from Russia.

French citizens must be at least 18 years old to serve in the military, and service for men and women is voluntary. In 2019, however, President Emmanuel Macron's government announced a new mandatory civil service program for teenagers. Young people could choose a variety of service options, including teaching and working with charities, along with more traditional military service preparation.

France spent the equivalent of approximately $58.7 billion on defense in 2021.[3]

Almost all of France's defense weapons systems are made in France; it can manufacture all its needed air, land, and naval weapons. France was a founding member of NATO in 1949. This is a multinational organization that works toward the peace and security of its members. In 2022, France continued to participate in NATO.

CHAPTER SEVEN

ECONOMICS

France is one of the leading economic powers in the world. It ranks among countries such as Japan, Germany, and the United States. France has rich resources and productive industries, and the country attracts millions of tourists every year. France is a capitalist country, but it strives for socioeconomic equality through policies, taxes, and social spending. France has large private companies. These include Air France, which is an airline; France Telecom, a telecommunications company; and Renault Group, an auto manufacturer. The government, however, maintains a controlling presence in some economic sectors, such as the power, public transportation, and defense industries.

By law, a standard French workweek is 35 hours long.

France exported $746 billion worth of goods in 2020 and imported $803 billion in goods.[1] Its main export items were aircraft, cars and vehicle parts, gas turbines, and wine. France is known for producing other items, including jewelry, perfume, and cheese. France's major imports are cars, crude petroleum, refined petroleum, and aircraft machinery. The country's main trading partners include Germany, the United States, Italy, Spain, and the United Kingdom.

France's estimated gross domestic product (GDP) in 2020 was more than $2.8 trillion, which was the ninth-highest in the world.[2] France had more than 30 million people in the workforce in 2020.[3] The unemployment rate in 2019 was 8.4 percent, and that worsened the following year due to the COVID-19 pandemic.[4] In 2018, 13.6 percent of the population lived below the poverty line.[5]

NATURAL RESOURCES

An important sector of France's economy is agriculture, including forestry. Agriculture accounts for approximately 3 percent of France's labor force. It contributes about 2 percent to the country's GDP.[6] Though it may not sound like a lot, it means France is Europe's leading agricultural nation.

France has nearly 74 million acres (30 million ha) devoted to agriculture.[7] Some of France's most important crops include sugar beets, potatoes, rapeseed, and grains such as wheat, corn, and barley. France accounts for approximately one-third of the EU's production of oilseeds, cereals, and wines.[9] France is the most famous wine-making country in the world. Regions of France with vineyards that produce popular wines include Champagne, Burgundy, and Bordeaux. France produces other fruits, including apples, pears, and peaches, and some animal products, such as pork, milk, and cheese.

Timber is another important natural resource. France has more than 57,000 square miles (148,000 sq km) of woodland. The forestry industry employs more than 80,000 people.[10]

MANUFACTURING

France's manufacturing base includes automobile, chemical, aircraft, electronics, food, and textile industries. Approximately 19.5 percent of France's labor force is involved in manufacturing, mining, and industry.[11] The car manufacturing companies Renault and Peugeot dominate the French automotive industry.

France is the biggest sawn hardwood producer in Europe.

Together, the two companies produce and sell millions of cars worldwide. The automobile industry provides many jobs. It also supports additional industries in the country, including tire manufacturers and other related fields. France also manufactures aircraft, as well as railway locomotives for the expanding high-speed train market.

France's metal industry produces steel and aluminum. The country also makes a variety of professional electronics, including radar equipment. The country's main mineral resources are potash, sodium chloride, and sulfur.

The chemical industry includes the manufacture of chemicals, pharmaceuticals, and perfumes. France is particularly well known for its perfumes. The Caron perfume house in Paris is 100 years old. Other famous brands include Chanel and Dior.

The food and beverage industries represent a large portion of France's manufacturing. Wine and champagne are important export products. France produces other ready-to-eat foods, including foie gras and mustard. France has one of the world's largest food and beverage industries.

SERVICE INDUSTRY

France's service industry is a significant part of its economy. It represented a little more than 71 percent of France's GDP in 2020.[12] Approximately 77 percent of the nation's labor force is involved in the service sector.[13] Service jobs include work in a variety of fields, such as retail, health care, education, banking, and finance.

Tourism has long been a significant part of France's service industry. France's beautiful landscapes, famous museums and cultural showpieces, and renowned food and wine attract visitors from around the world. France is one of the world's most visited countries, and it has the third-largest income from tourism in the world. The tourism industry alone employs approximately 10 percent of France's workforce and contributes about 9 percent to the country's GDP.[14]

ENERGY AND TRANSPORTATION

France uses a variety of energy sources to meet its needs, including fossil fuels, nuclear power, and renewables. In 2019, 90 percent of France's electricity generation came from nuclear and

France has relied on imported oil for decades. In 2020, it used more than one million barrels of oil a day.

renewable energy. Both sources are considered to have low- or zero-carbon emissions. That means they give off either low or no amounts of greenhouse gases that contribute to global warming. The rest of France's electricity, some 10 percent, was supplied by fossil fuels and other sources.[15]

France is dependent on imports for its oil consumption. The country has a major oil-refining industry to process the crude oil it imports. France has a network of pipelines to deliver gas, oil, and refined products. France's main oil suppliers are Kazakhstan, Saudi Arabia, and Russia. In March 2022, in response to Russia's invasion of Ukraine, France's prime minister declared plans to end gas and oil imports from Russia by 2027.

Nuclear power supplied almost three-fourths of France's electricity in 2019.[16] That is the highest proportion of energy generated by nuclear power in the world. Nuclear power, however, is controversial because it produces radioactive waste that must be managed for thousands of years. As a result, President Emmanuel Macron pledged to reduce reliance on nuclear energy to 50 percent by 2035.

In 2022, France had 56 nuclear reactors.

France greatly expanded its use of renewable energy sources in the 2000s. These included solar, wind, and hydropower. France's Cestas Solar Park is one of Europe's largest solar power stations.

France's transportation infrastructure includes roads and highways, railways, and airports. In addition, France has five major seaports. The country's extensive road system totals more than 620,000 miles (1 million km). A network of 18,417 miles (29,640 km) of railways connects cities throughout France, as well as France to other nations.[17] One high-speed passenger train runs between Paris, Lyon, and the Mediterranean coast. Other trains link Paris to London in just three hours and carry millions of travelers each year. These trains cross from France to England through an undersea tunnel that connects the European continent and Great Britain.

France has hundreds of international and domestic airports. The two main airports are Charles de Gaulle and Orly, both located near Paris. More than a dozen registered air carriers in France serve passengers and transport cargo.

More than 26 million people went through the Charles de Gaulle Airport in 2021.

CHAPTER EIGHT

FRANCE TODAY

On average, French people are educated and literate and have a high standard of living. Many speak a foreign language and enjoy travel. French people work hard, but they leave time to relax with family and friends and enjoy cultural and recreational activities.

The United Nations is an international organization. It strives to bring security and peace to the globe. The United Nations ranks France's performance in human development achievements above average compared with other very high-ranking countries, such as

Many French citizens are proud to belong to a country with a rich history and a promising future.

Germany, the United Kingdom, and the United States. This development achievement measures a country's human progress.

The World Bank is an international banking organization. It classifies France as a wealthy, high-income nation. In general, France's economic growth as measured by GDP has been stable since the 1960s. However, like many countries dealing with the fallout of the COVID-19 pandemic, France's GDP dropped in 2020. French citizens benefit from social services provided by the government, including health care, education, and pensions for retirement.

RECREATION AND LEISURE

The French put an emphasis on a good work-life balance, and this is reinforced by the government. Laws limit work to 35 hours a week—which is lower than the standard 40-hour workweek in the United States—and prohibit employers from requiring employees to read work emails on the weekends. In addition, French people get five weeks of vacation

HUMAN DEVELOPMENT ACHIEVEMENTS

The Human Development Report is published each year by the United Nations Development Programme. It ranks countries using indicators such as life expectancy at birth, adult literacy rate, per capita income, human resource development, and basic needs such as freedom and dignity. In 2020, France ranked twenty-sixth out of 189 countries and territories.[1] According to the report, France ranks very high in human development. The country's average measures of basic human development achievements have risen steadily since 1990.

from work each year, and they get almost a dozen public holidays off. The short workweek and days off leave time for leisure, hobbies, and recreation.

For many people, evenings are for sit-down family meals, doing homework, and relaxing. Weekends are for family, friends, and cultural and recreational pursuits. Many French people enjoy long afternoons sitting in a café reading or talking with friends. Many go to movies and attend theaters. French people fill museums, art galleries, historic monuments, and cultural sites along with tourists.

French people also enjoy more active forms of recreation and sports. France has a well-maintained network of paths and trails for walking and jogging. National and regional parks attract hikers and campers. French people enjoy popular seaside resorts, such as Saint-Tropez and Cannes, as much as foreign tourists.

Millions of French people ski and visit resorts in the Alps and Pyrenees in the winter. Other popular sports in France include tennis and soccer. One traditional French game people often enjoy is called *boules*. To play this game, people roll or

OLYMPICS IN FRANCE

France has hosted the Olympic Games many times. In both 1900 and 1924, it held the Summer Games. In 1924, 1968, and 1992, it hosted the Winter Games. The country got ready to hold another Summer Olympics in 2024 in Paris—exactly 100 years after its last Summer Games. France promised the first gender-balanced and carbon-neutral Olympics ever. The Games also planned to feature a new sport called breaking, which is a competitive form of break dancing.

throw a ball with the goal of getting it close to a target ball. They also try to knock their opponents' balls off course.

EDUCATION

France has a good reputation for its well-developed education system. France boasts an overall adult literacy rate of at least 99 percent.[2] French children are required to attend school from ages six to 16. Some children start as young as three years old in preprimary school. France has both public and private educational institutions. Public schools are free, and they follow a national curriculum. Many private schools are Roman Catholic. The government pays for a portion of the tuition to private school. The school year for French children begins in September and ends in June.

French children ages six to ten receive elementary education in primary school. Secondary education is for ages 11 to 18. The first two years of secondary school are similar to middle school in the United States. Students study French, foreign languages, math, history, geography, life and earth science, physics, chemistry, art, technology, and physical education. Later in secondary school, students eventually choose between a vocational, technological, or academic course of study. All tracks can lead to university studies, though the technological and vocational courses also prepare students to enter the job market in their chosen fields. At the end of secondary school, students take a national exam that may earn them a spot at a university.

French students go to school from September until June and get many educational opportunities.

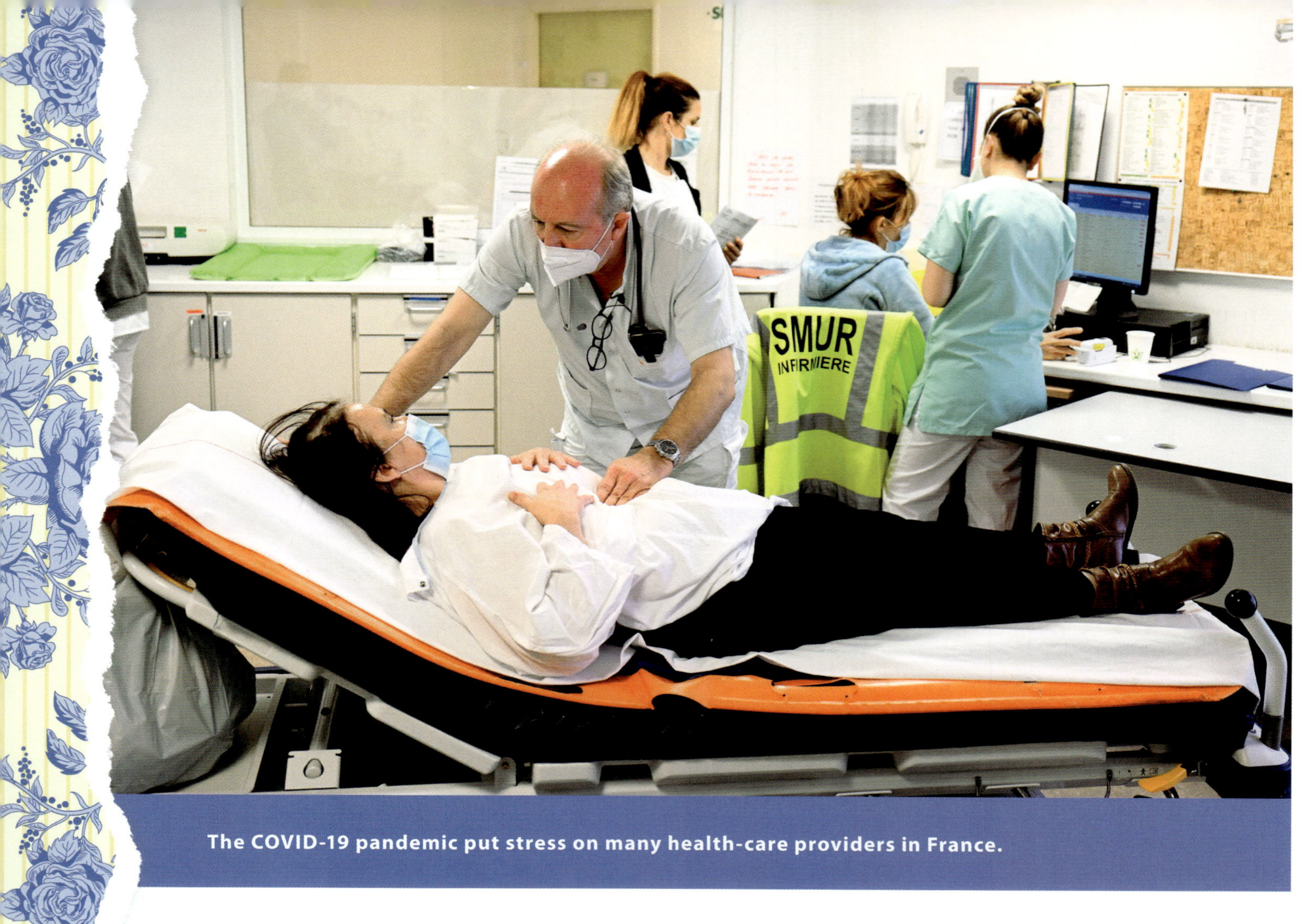

The COVID-19 pandemic put stress on many health-care providers in France.

France has both private and public universities. Public universities are affordable for many residents. They offer two- and four-year programs focusing on a variety of studies. Some universities offer two-year technical degrees. These degrees can be used to enter the job market or to prepare for a four-year university program leading to a bachelor's degree. Students who graduate may continue their education at graduate and professional schools. There, they work to earn master's and doctorate degrees.

HEALTH

On average, French people enjoy good health compared with people in other developed nations. In addition, some people consider France's health-care system to be one of the best in the world. Like many countries, though, France and its people suffered poor health outcomes during the COVID-19 pandemic, which began in 2020.

Life expectancy in France is among the highest in all of Europe. In 2019, before the pandemic, the majority of French adults reported being in good health. Fewer French people died of preventable and treatable causes than across the EU. All French people—both urban and rural—have access to clean drinking water, which is another important factor in their good health outcomes.

The main causes of death in France are heart disease, stroke, and lung cancer. According to data in 2019, approximately 33 percent of all health-related deaths in France were due to behavioral risk factors, such as tobacco smoking, diet, alcohol consumption, and low physical activity. Smoking rates in France have fallen over the past two decades, but almost one-quarter of adults still smoked daily in 2019. Alcohol consumption also has decreased among the French, but it is still more than 10 percent higher than the EU average.[3]

During the pandemic, many people in France wore face masks in public.

Obesity rates have increased in France, but they are comparable to the rates in most EU countries. French 15-year-olds, however, are less physically active than their European peers. In 2018, 90 percent reported not doing at least moderate physical activity every day, which was second only to Italy.[4]

Health care in France is high quality and affordable. French people have good access to primary care physicians and specialists. Health care is provided to all legal residents, but it is not entirely free. It is funded by a combination of public and private money. While the state covers much of the cost of health care, some services must be paid for out of pocket. Therefore, French law requires that all residents be covered by some form of private health insurance. In general, France has plenty of hospital beds and physicians for its citizens, though the health-care system was strained by the COVID-19 pandemic.

THE COVID-19 PANDEMIC

Despite good overall health and access to care, France was one of the EU countries hit hardest by the COVID-19 pandemic. Common symptoms of the disease were chills, fever, coughing, tiredness, body aches, headaches, sore throats, and a loss of smell or taste. Other symptoms included chest pain and difficulty breathing. The majority of people who contracted COVID-19 recovered after a few weeks, but others needed prolonged medical attention. In France, the country's high life expectancy rate dropped temporarily in 2020 because of deaths due to COVID-19.

The French government tried to control the spread of the disease. It did this in part by putting the country in lockdown. That meant no large social gatherings could take place and only essential businesses could stay open. The majority of people were told to go home and stay there. As a result of the pandemic, many French people's mental health suffered. Levels of anxiety and depression in 2020 were double what they were in 2017. By June 2022, more than 149,000 people in France had died due to COVID-19.[5]

The pandemic demonstrated that despite the many strengths of France's national health-care system, it had weaknesses too. For instance, the country's complex health-care system made it hard for different parts of the system to coordinate medical responses with one another. Going forward, the country had the opportunity to learn

In 2020 alone, approximately 65,000 French people died of COVID-19. That accounted for almost 10 percent of all deaths in the country.[6]

from the COVID-19 pandemic and potentially change its practices in order to tackle future pandemics. The result could be an even better health-care system in France.

CHALLENGES FOR THE FUTURE

The ongoing COVID-19 pandemic was one challenge facing France in the 2020s, but it was far from the only one. The country also faced the threat of climate change. At the time, global warming was already affecting snow and ice cover in France's high mountains. France's largest glacier, called the Mer de Glace, was shrinking by more than 16.4 feet (5 m) each year.[7] Alpine plants and animals were losing habitats as the mountainsides warmed. France's government was committed to limiting global warming. In fact, it was in Paris in 2015 that world leaders at the United Nations Climate Change Conference agreed to take measures to limit global warming. The international agreement they signed is commonly known as the Paris Climate Agreement.

France also faces challenges as a multicultural nation. Immigrants make up about 10 percent of France's population.[8] Many people have come to live in France from neighboring countries, such as Portugal,

Many people in France have participated in rallies to bring awareness to climate change.

Italy, and Spain. More recent immigrants have arrived from Africa and Asia. France has Europe's largest Muslim community and has been criticized at times for not making the population feel welcome. For instance, in 2004, France passed a controversial law that forbade students from wearing any obvious religious symbols in public schools, including large Christian crosses, Jewish skullcaps, and Islamic headscarves. In 2010, face coverings were banned, including burkas worn by some Muslim women. Six years after that, Mediterranean resorts in France banned burkinis, or body-covering beachwear. Many Muslims view these policies as discriminatory, though French leaders say the laws are needed to protect France's strict separation of church and state.

France also has to contend with hate crimes. These crimes target people based on their religion, race, gender, or sexual orientation. Incidents of hate crimes can include property damage, assault, or any type of threat. By 2020, homophobic insults and attacks were on the rise in France.

Transgender, Jewish, and Muslim people, as well as people living in France from other countries, were targets of hate crimes too.

The health of the economy was also something on French people's minds. President Emmanuel Macron proposed economic reforms that were designed to increase the country's economic growth, decrease national debt, and provide more private investment opportunities. Not all the reforms, however, were popular with French citizens. In 2018, transportation workers went on strike to protest plans to privatize the state-run railway company. That same year, protesters wearing yellow vests took to the streets because of proposed fuel-tax increases. In 2020, thousands of people marched to protest changes to the pension system, which they worried would require people to work longer before receiving retirement benefits.

France is in a good position to address its challenges and continue to be a world leader in the future. It is stable, and many people agree that it is a generally well-run country. Not only is it economically well-off but France is also rich in tradition and culture and continues to influence the world today.

ESSENTIAL FACTS

OFFICIAL NAME: FRENCH REPUBLIC

GEOGRAPHY

Area: 212,935 square miles (551,500 sq km) of metropolitan France

Highest Elevation: Mont Blanc in the Alps at 15,771 feet (4,807 m)

Lowest Elevation: Rhône River delta at −7 feet (−2 m)

PEOPLE

Population: 68.3 million (2022 est.)

Most Populous City: Paris (2.1 million)

Ethnic Groups: Mostly Celtic and Latin; also minority groups of Teutonic, Slavic, North African, Indo-Chinese, Basque; overseas departments include Chinese, Amerindian, East Indian

Religions: Catholicism, Islam, Protestantism, Buddhism, Judaism

GOVERNMENT

Type of Government: Republic

Capital: Paris

Head of State: President

Head of Government: Prime minister

Legislature: Bicameral, with a Senate and a National Assembly

ECONOMY

Currency: Euro

Major Industries: Machinery, chemicals, automobiles, tourism

Natural Resources: Coal, iron ore, hardwood

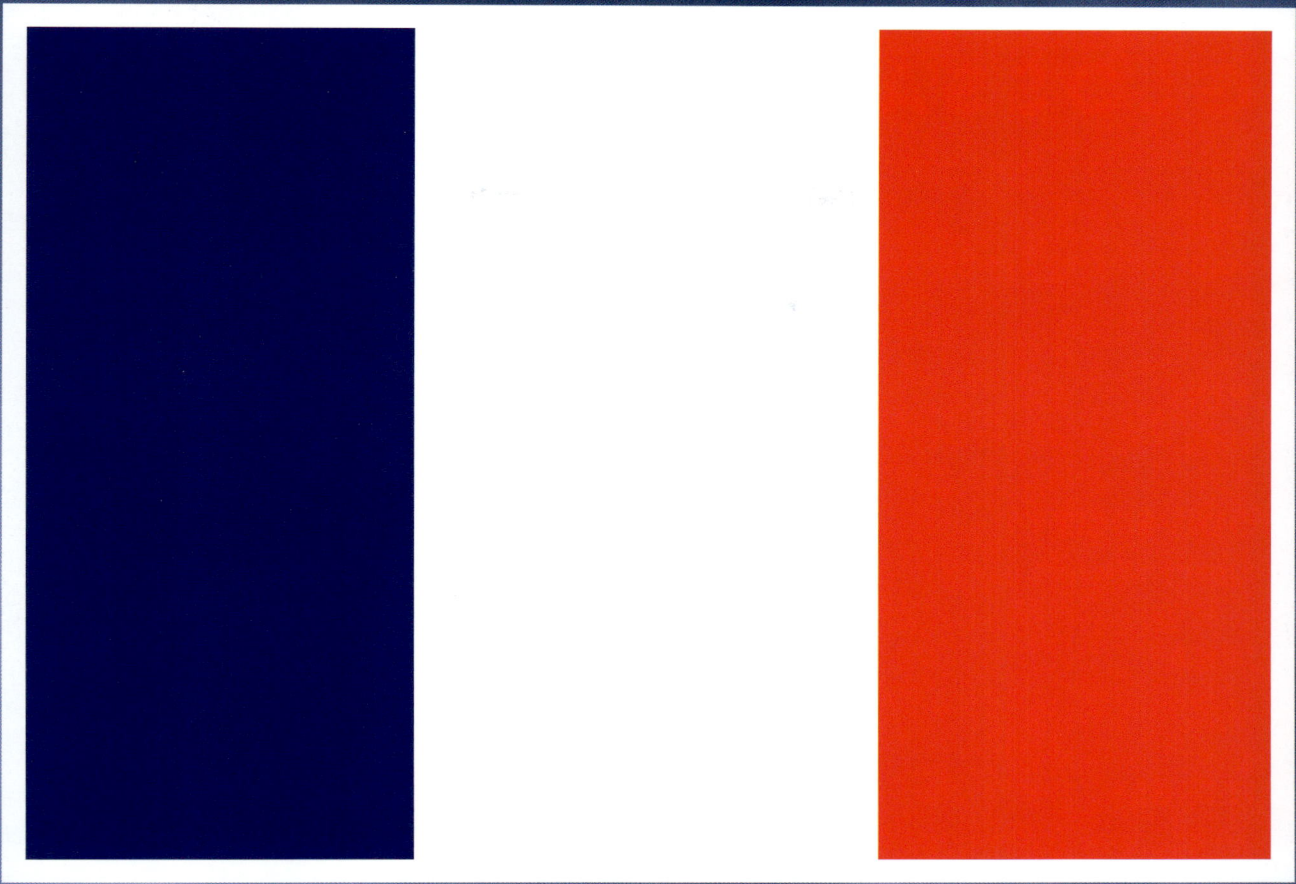

NATIONAL SYMBOLS

National Anthem: "La Marseillaise" ("The Marseillaise")

National Bird: Gallic rooster

National Flower: Lily

GLOSSARY

ALLY

A country that works with one or more other countries toward the same goal, often in a time of war.

ALPINE

Relating to high mountains.

BIODIVERSITY

The many different plants and animals in an ecosystem.

BURKA

A loose garment that covers the body and face.

BUTTRESS

An architectural feature that strengthens or provides support for a building or structure.

CATACOMBS

Underground networks of rooms and tunnels used for burial.

EUROPEAN UNION (EU)

A group of European countries that work together to encourage economic and political cooperation.

GROSS DOMESTIC PRODUCT (GDP)
The monetary value of all final goods and services produced within a nation's geographic borders over a specified period of time.

INFRASTRUCTURE
The physical structures, such as roads, railways, and power plants, that make it possible for a city or nation to function.

NEOLITHIC
Relating to the period beginning in approximately 10,000 BCE when people started farming but still used stone tools.

PLATEAU
An area of level ground that is higher than the surrounding area.

SANCTION
An action taken to punish a country or force it to follow international laws.

SECTOR
A distinct part of a nation's economy.

ADDITIONAL RESOURCES

SELECTED BIBLIOGRAPHY

Averbuck, Alexis, et al. *Lonely Planet France*. Lonely Planet, 2021.

"France." *CIA World Factbook*, 11 Apr. 2022, cia.gov. Accessed 14 Apr. 2022.

Bernard, François, et al. "France." *Encyclopedia Britannica*, 13 Apr. 2022, britannica.com. Accessed 14 Apr. 2022.

FURTHER READINGS

Hammond, Francis. *Versailles: A Private Invitation*. Flammarion, 2018.

Parks, Peggy J. *Growing Up in France*. ReferencePoint, 2018.

Peyrel, Benjamin. *The Eiffel Tower*. Abrams, 2020.

ONLINE RESOURCES

To learn more about France, please visit **abdobooklinks.com** or scan this QR code. These links are routinely monitored and updated to provide the most current information available.

MORE INFORMATION

For more information on this subject, contact or visit the following organizations:

Embassy of France in the United States
4101 Reservoir Rd. NW
Washington, DC 20007
franceintheus.org
The French Embassy in the United States offers current news and information for people interested in visiting, moving to, or studying in France.

Louvre Museum
Rue de Rivoli
75001 Paris, France
louvre.fr/en
The Louvre Museum in Paris is one of the most popular art museums in the world. It houses works from ancient times to the 1800s.

Palace of Versailles
Place d'Armes
78000 Versailles, France
en.chateauversailles.fr
Visitors can book tours to see the Palace of Versailles and explore the stunning rooms and gardens that span more than 1,975 acres (800 ha).

SOURCE NOTES

CHAPTER 1. A TOUR OF FRANCE
1. Alexis Averbuck et al. *Lonely Planet France.* Lonely Planet, 2021. 77–78.
2. "France." *CIA World Factbook*, 15 June 2022, cia.gov. Accessed 20 June 2022.
3. Averbuck et al., *Lonely Planet France*, 76–77.
4. "The Origin of the Eiffel Tower." *Mental Floss*, 6 May 2008, mentalfloss.com. Accessed 20 June 2022.
5. Pascale Filliâtre. "9 Fascinating Facts about the Chateau de Chambord." *Explore France*, 19 Dec. 2019, us.france.fr. Accessed 20 June 2022.
6. "Corse." *City Population*, n.d., citypopulation.de. Accessed 20 June 2022.

CHAPTER 2. GEOGRAPHY
1. "France." *CIA World Factbook*, 15 June 2022, cia.gov. Accessed 20 June 2022.
2. François Bernard et al. "France." *Encyclopedia Britannica*, 15 June 2022, britannica.com. Accessed 20 June 2022.
3. Damian Carrington. "Two-Thirds of Glacier Ice in the Alps 'Will Melt by 2100.'" *Guardian*, 9 Apr. 2019, theguardian.com. Accessed 20 June 2022.
4. Bernard et al., "France."
5. "Mont Blanc." *Encyclopedia Britannica*, 5 Dec. 2018, britannica.com. Accessed 20 June 2022.
6. "France." *CIA World Factbook*.
7. Aubrey Diem. "Rhône River." *Encyclopedia Britannica*, 3 Nov. 2015, britannica.com. Accessed 20 June 2022.
8. "Lake Geneva." *Lake Geneva Switzerland*, n.d., lake-geneva-switzerland.com. Accessed 20 June 2022.
9. "Garonne River." *Encyclopedia Britannica*, 24 June 2010, britannica.com. Accessed 20 June 2022.
10. "France." *CIA World Factbook*.
11. Bernard et al., "France."
12. "Climate and Average Weather Year Round in Strasbourg." *Weather Spark*, n.d., weatherspark.com. Accessed 20 June 2022.
13. Bernard et al., "France."
14. "Mistral." *Encyclopedia Britannica*, 21 Nov. 2018, britannica.com. Accessed 20 June 2022.
15. "Mount Pelée." *Encyclopedia Britannica*, 5 Apr. 2016, britannica.com. Accessed 20 June 2022.

CHAPTER 3. PLANTS AND ANIMALS

1. "France's Biodiversity at Risk." *IUCN Red List*, May 2013, iucn.org. Accessed 20 June 2022.
2. Anna Savolainen. "One in Four Species in France Is Endangered, Despite Biodiversity Protection Efforts." *Climate Scorecard*, 17 June 2020, climatescorecard.org. Accessed 20 June 2022.
3. "France's Biodiversity at Risk."
4. Alexis Averbuck et al. *Lonely Planet France*. Lonely Planet, 2021. 969.
5. Averbuck et al., *Lonely Planet France*, 969.
6. Blandine Prigent. "Discover France's 11 National Parks." *Explore France*, 24 June 2020, uk.france.fr. Accessed 20 June 2022.
7. Ceil Miller Bouchet. "The Best UNESCO World Heritage Sites in France." *National Geographic*, 1 June 2016, nationalgeographic.com. Accessed 20 June 2022.
8. "Pyrénées—Mont Perdu." *UNESCO World Heritage Convention*, n.d., whc.unesco.org. Accessed 20 June 2022.
9. Savolainen, "One in Four Species in France Is Endangered."
10. "France's Biodiversity at Risk."
11. "Biodiversité." *Data Lab*, 2018, statistiques.developpement-durable.gouv.fr. Accessed 20 June 2022.
12. Savolainen, "One in Four Species in France Is Endangered."
13. "Biodiversité."

CHAPTER 4. HISTORY

1. "Marie Antoinette and the French Revolution." *PBS*, n.d., pbs.org. Accessed 20 June 2022.
2. "Liberty, Equality, Fraternity." *France in the United States*, 30 Nov. 2007, franceintheus.org. Accessed 20 June 2022.
3. François Bernard et al. "France." *Encyclopedia Britannica*, 15 June 2022, britannica.com. Accessed 20 June 2022.
4. Michael Ray. "Paris Attacks of 2015." *Encyclopedia Britannica*, 15 Apr. 2022, britannica.com. Accessed 20 June 2022.

CHAPTER 5. PEOPLE AND CULTURE

1. "France." *CIA World Factbook*, 15 June 2022, cia.gov. Accessed 20 June 2022.
2. Kimberly Daul. "Paris." *Encyclopedia Britannica*, 10 Sept. 2021, britannica.com. Accessed 20 June 2022.
3. "French Language History." *Today Translations*, n.d., todaytranslations.com. Accessed 20 June 2022.
4. "France." *CIA World Factbook*.
5. *Ice Age Artists*. National Geographic, 2021. 49.
6. "Number of Visitors to the Louvre in Paris from 2007 to 2020." *Statista*, 5 Aug. 2021, statista.com. Accessed 20 June 2022.
7. Alexis Averbuck et al. *Lonely Planet France*. Lonely Planet, 2021. 952.

CHAPTER 6. POLITICS

1. "France." *CIA World Factbook*, 15 June 2022, cia.gov. Accessed 20 June 2022.
2. "France." *CIA World Factbook*.
3. Lucie Jeudy. "Expenditure on Defense in France from 2014 to 2021." *Statista*, 1 Mar. 2022, statista.com. Accessed 20 June 2022.

CHAPTER 7. ECONOMICS

1. "France." *CIA World Factbook*, 15 June 2022, cia.gov. Accessed 20 June 2022.
2. "France." *CIA World Factbook*.
3. "France—Labor Force, Total." *Trading Economics*, n.d., tradingeconomics.com. Accessed 20 June 2022.
4. Aaron O'Neill. "France: Unemployment Rate from 1991 to 2021." *Statista*, 7 June 2022, statista.com. Accessed 20 June 2022.
5. "France." *CIA World Factbook*.
6. François Bernard et al. "France." *Encyclopedia Britannica*, 15 June 2022, britannica.com. Accessed 20 June 2022.
7. Bernard et al., "France."
8. Eloise Trenda. "French Wine Exports by Destination, in Market Share Value in 2020." *Statista*, 8 Nov. 2021, statista.com. Accessed 20 June 2022.
9. Bernard et al., "France."
10. Bernard et al., "France."
11. "France." *CIA World Factbook*.
12. Aaron O'Neill. "France: Distribution of Gross Domestic Product (GDP) across Economic Sectors from 2010 to 2020." *Statista*, 15 Feb. 2022, statista.com. Accessed 20 June 2022.
13. "France." *CIA World Factbook*.
14. Bernard et al., "France."
15. "France." *IAEA*, 2018, iaea.org. Accessed 20 June 2022.
16. "France." *IAEA*.
17. "France." *CIA World Factbook*.

CHAPTER 8. FRANCE TODAY

1. "France." *Human Development Report*, 2020, hdr.undp.org. Accessed 20 June 2022.
2. "France Literacy Rate 1990–2022." *Macro Trends*, n.d., macrotrends.net. Accessed 20 June 2022.
3. "France: Country Health Profile 2021." *OECD*, 2021, oecd-ilibrary.org. Accessed 20 June 2022.
4. "France: Country Health Profile 2021."
5. "France." *Reuters COVID-19 Tracker*, n.d., graphics.reuters.com. Accessed 20 June 2022.
6. "France: Country Health Profile 2021."
7. "Glacier Case." *International Rights of Nature Tribunal*, n.d., rightsofnaturetribunal.org. Accessed 20 June 2022.
8. Martin Greenacre. "Immigration in France: What Are the Real Numbers?" *Local*, 15 Oct. 2021, thelocal.fr. Accessed 20 June 2022.
9. "Macron: France Will Respond without Weakness to Russia's 'Act of War' on Ukraine." *Reuters*, 24 Feb. 2022, reuters.com. Accessed 20 June 2022.

INDEX

YVETTE LaPIERRE

Yvette LaPierre lives in North Dakota with her family. She writes and edits books and articles for children and adults. LaPierre took a high school trip to France very much like the one described in the first chapter.